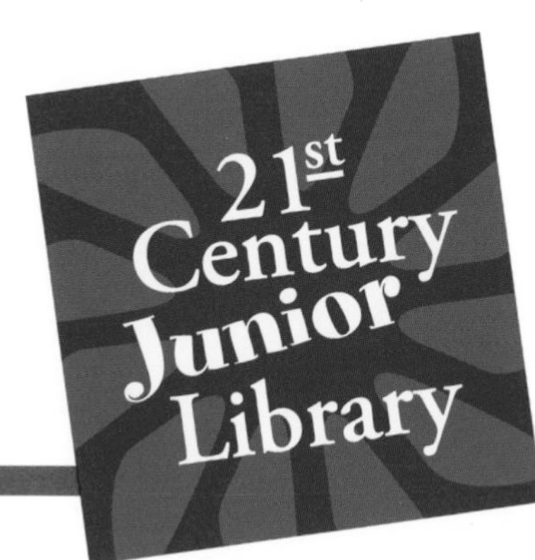

WORKING AT A TV STATION

by Lucia Raatma

CHERRY LAKE PUBLISHING * ANN ARBOR, MICHIGAN

Published in the United States of America by Cherry Lake Publishing
Ann Arbor, Michigan
www.cherrylakepublishing.com

Content Adviser: Jeff Forster, Vice President of Production and Station Enterprises, Detroit Public Television

Photo Credits: Cover and page 8, ©withGod/Shutterstock, Inc.; cover and page 10, ©Paul Yates/Shutterstock, Inc.; cover and page 16, ©Linqong/Dreamstime.com; cover and page 20, ©Gabivali/Dreamstime.com; page 4, ©iStockphoto.com/DOConnell; page 6, ©Dennis Sabo/Shutterstock, Inc.; page 12, ©kldy/Shutterstock, Inc.; page 14, ©ArrowStudio, LLC/Shutterstock, Inc.; page 18, ©Photographerlondon/Dreamstime.com

LIBRARY OF CONGRESS CATALOGING-IN-PUBLICATION DATA

Raatma, Lucia.
Working at a TV station/by Lucia Raatma.
p. cm.—(21st century junior library)
Includes bibliographical references and index.
ISBN-13: 978-1-60279-980-6 (lib. bdg.)
ISBN-10: 1-60279-980-6 (lib. bdg.)
1. Television broadcasting—Juvenile literature. 2. Television stations—Juvenile literature. 3. Television stations—Employees—Juvenile literature. 4. Television—Vocational guidance—Juvenile literature. I. Title.
PN1992.57.R32 2011
384.55—dc22 2010029985

Cherry Lake Publishing would like to acknowledge the work of The Partnership for 21st Century Skills. Please visit www.21stcenturyskills.org *for more information.*

Printed in the United States of America
Corporate Graphics Inc.
January 2011
CLSP08

CONTENTS

Have you ever wondered where your favorite TV shows are made?

What Is a TV Station?

Will you need a coat today? What will the weather be like? Your mom turns on the TV to find out. A news show has the information you need. Many people work on the news show.

Some shows are recorded on sets in the TV station.
This is the set for a talk show.

Most TV shows you watch are **broadcast** from TV stations. They are recorded and then shown later.

News shows are **live**. The people on TV are talking at the same time you hear them. They work at a TV station.

Think about the TV shows you watch. What do you learn from them? Are any of them live? Do you think any were recorded at another time?

Directors may need to keep an eye on several cameras at once.

TV Station Workers

Many people work at a TV station. You may not see most of them on your screen. They work behind the scenes. One important person is the **director**. She decides how each show is put together. She tells people where to sit and stand.

Videographers use cameras to broadcast events such as sports on TV.

The **producer** asks guests to be on the show. She decides what stories to cover. **Reporters** cover the news stories. **Videographers** record them with cameras. There might be a big fire in your town. Maybe a big football game is being played. People want to see these events on TV.

Do you know people who are reporters or writers? Ask them about the stories they work on. Where do they get their ideas? How do they make sure the stories are true?

Helicopters with cameras can help get news stories on the air quickly.

Some TV station workers drive vans. Others fly helicopters! They help reporters and videographers get from place to place. They also carry cameras, microphones, and other equipment.

Writers and editors work together to make news stories the best they can be.

Writers and **editors** work on the news stories. They make the stories fit into the right amount of time. News **anchors** sit in front of the cameras. They read the stories to everyone watching.

Write a news story about an event in your neighborhood. Then get together with your friends. Create your own news show. Two people can be news anchors. Another person can use a video camera to record the show!

Cameras capture the action of a TV show.

Meteorologists report on the weather. Other people talk about sports and traffic. **Technicians** run the lights. They also check the sound. **Graphic designers** create colorful pictures that you see on the screen. Production assistants help with the **teleprompter**.

Watch the graphics that go with news stories. There might be drawings, charts, or fancy writing. Do the graphic designs make the news more interesting?

Try making your own TV show with friends.

Do You Want to Work at a TV Station?

Things happen fast at a TV station. Are you interested in working at one? You can start getting ready now! Practice your writing skills. Get used to talking in front of other people. Learn more about cameras and recording equipment.

One day you could be in front of the camera.

Ask a teacher if you can take a tour of a TV station. Learn what each person does. See what problems come up. Notice how workers solve those problems. You may want to be part of the action!

How many TV stations are in your town? How many people work at them? Go to their Web sites and see if you can find out. You may be surprised by how many people work at TV stations!

GLOSSARY

anchors (ANG-kurz) people who read the news on a TV show

broadcast (BRAWD-kast) sent out through TV or radio

director (duh-REK-tur) a person who supervises the action of a movie or TV show

editors (ED-uh-turz) people who review writing to make it better

graphic designers (GRAF-ik dih-ZINE-urz) people who create maps, charts, drawings, and other illustrations

live (LIVE) describing something that is broadcast as it's happening

meteorologists (MEE-tee-ur-OL-uh-jists) experts on the weather

producer (pruh-DOOSS-ur) a person in charge of a movie or TV show

reporters (ri-POR-turz) people who gather and report the news

technicians (tek-NISH-uhnz) people who work with specialized equipment

teleprompter (TELL-uh-prompt-ur) a machine that shows text for the news anchors to read

videographers (vid-ee-OG-ruh-furz) people who record sounds and pictures on video

FIND OUT MORE

BOOKS

Cupp, Dave, and Cecilia Minden. *TV-Station Secrets*. Mankato, MN: The Child's World, 2009.

Hutchings, Amy. *What Happens at a TV Station?* Pleasantville, NY: Weekly Reader Books, 2009.

WEB SITES

Kids Work!

www.knowitall.org/kidswork/etv/realpeople/index.html

Meet some real people who work at an educational TV station in South Carolina.

The Weather Channel Kids

www.theweatherchannelkids.com/

Learn more about what weather forecasters do. Play games, and get your local forecast!

INDEX

ABOUT THE AUTHOR

Lucia Raatma has written dozens of books for young readers. She and her family live in the Tampa Bay area of Florida. When she was growing up, her TV only showed three channels!